edible ensembles

GRETCHEN RÖEHRS

edible ensembles

A Fashion Feast for the Eyes

FROM BANANA PEEL JUMPSUITS
TO KALE FROCKS

RIZZOLI
NEW YORK

New York · Paris · London · Milan

*to eat it or to wear it —
that is the question*

red

TOMATO. STRAWBERRY. APPLE. RADISH.
WATERMELON. RASPBERRIES. CHERRY. LOBSTER.
CRANBERRY BEANS. MELON.

ceci n'est pas un dress

consider the lobster

(dress)

an apple a day   helps you strut & sashay

cherry bomb!

Sgt. Peppers Stylish
Pants Club

Simply
Radishing

ora-nge

HABANERO. ORANGE. CARROT. MANGO.
PEACH. PERSIMMON. PUMPKIN. CHEDDAR.

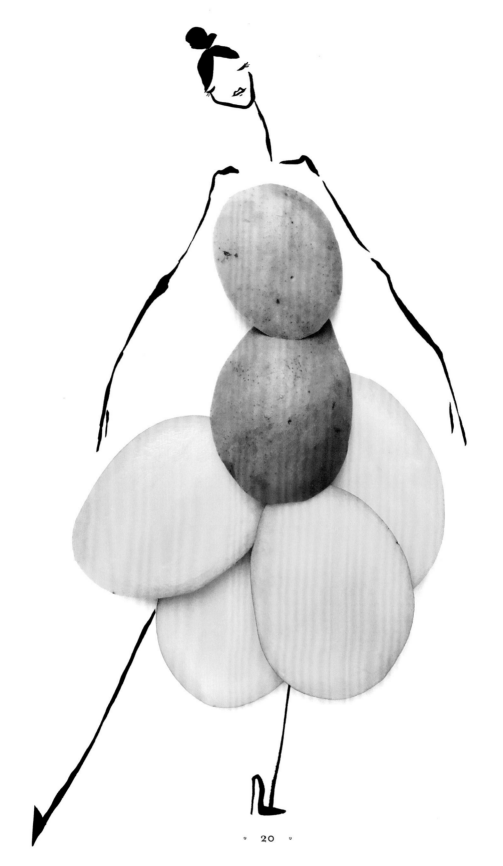

hello sunshine

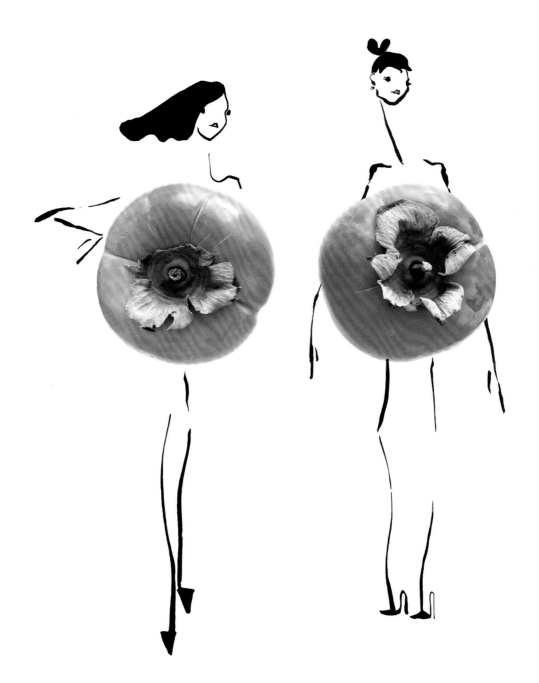

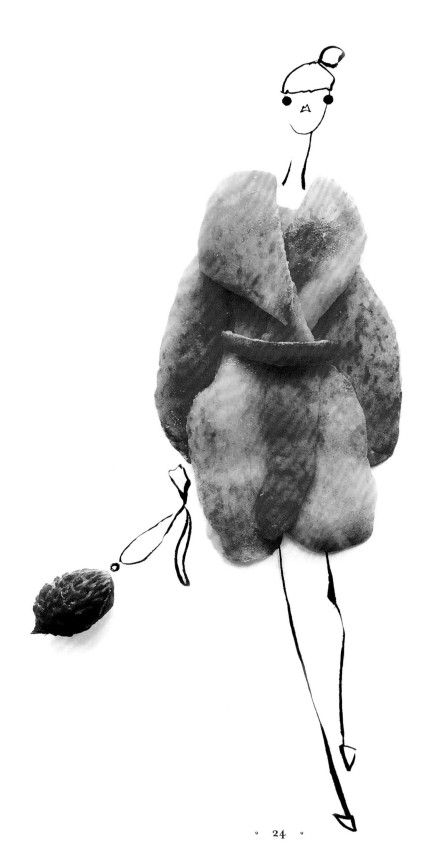

.yel

OW

BANANA. EGG. HONEYCOMB. CORN.
TORTELLINI. BUDDAH'S HAND. PINEAPPLE.
LEMON. SQUASH. CHANTERELLE.

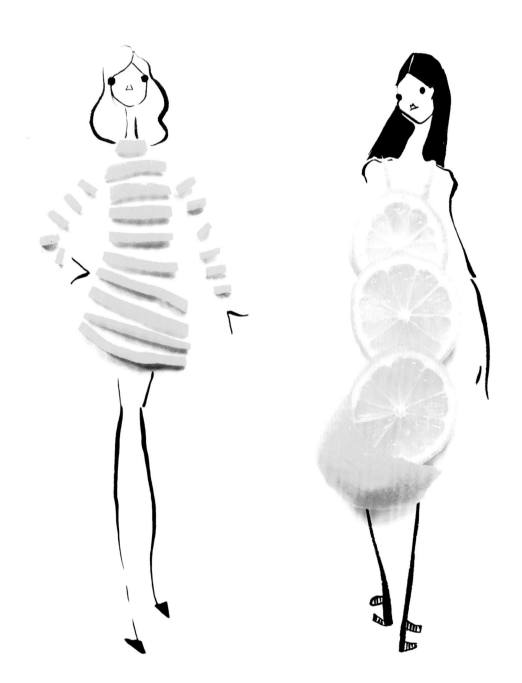

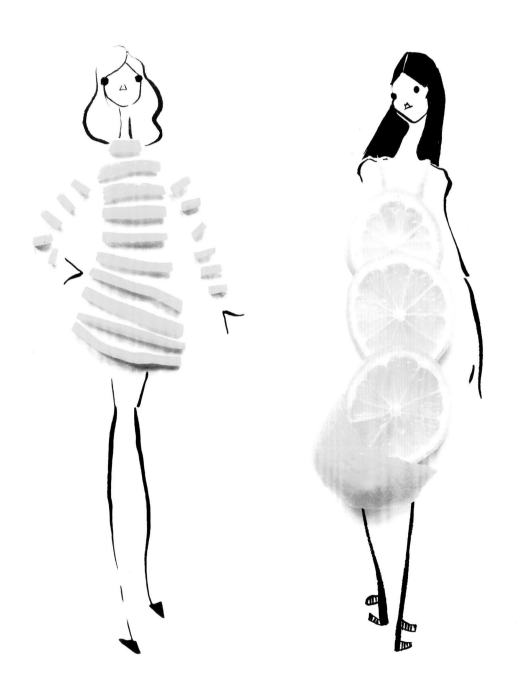

behold, eye candy!

Compost chic!

the breakfast of champignons

green

KALE. SWISS CHARD. BROCCOLI. ARTICHOKE.
TATSOI. FENNEL. LETTUCE. ROMANESCO. KIWI.
BRUSSELS SPROUTS. AVOCADO. CUCUMBER.
OLIVES. GRAPES. RADISH SHOOTS. TOMATILLO.
LIME. FIDDLEHEAD. SAGE.

dressing on the side, please!

chard on!

chard on!

does this plant
make me look fat?

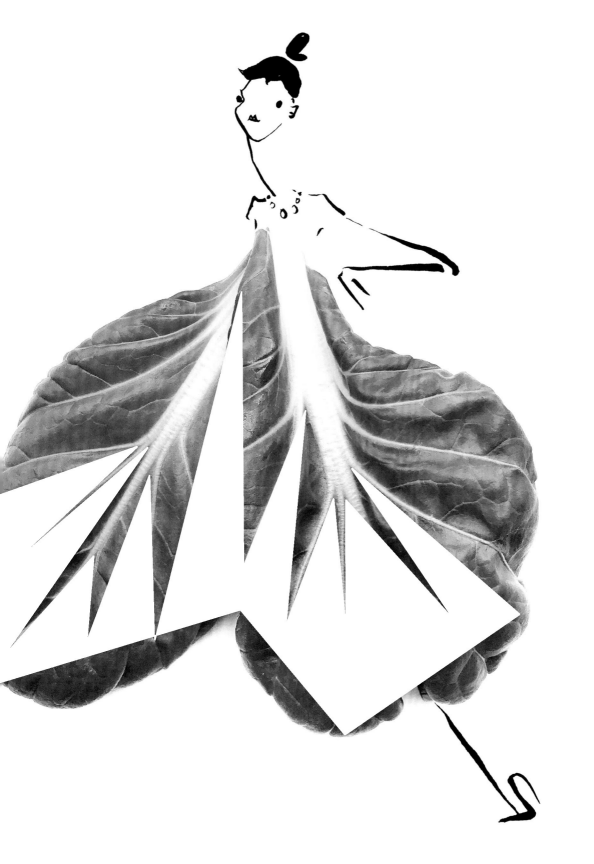

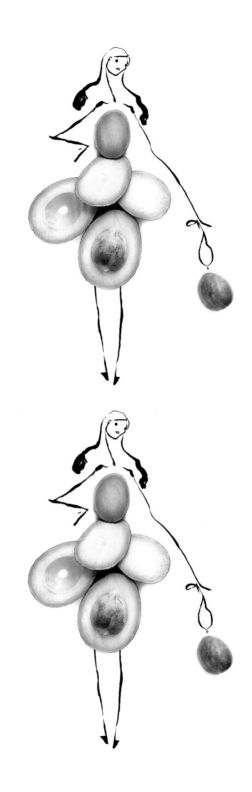

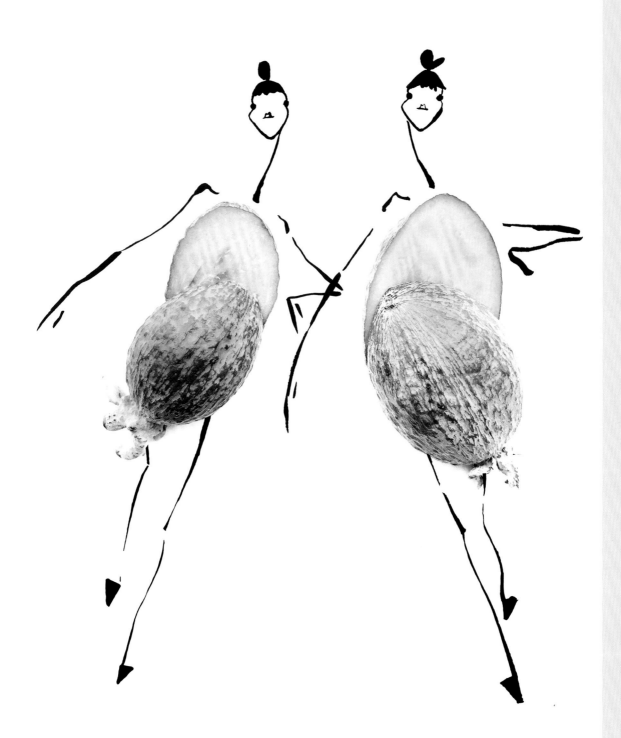

crudité crew

Sage, man

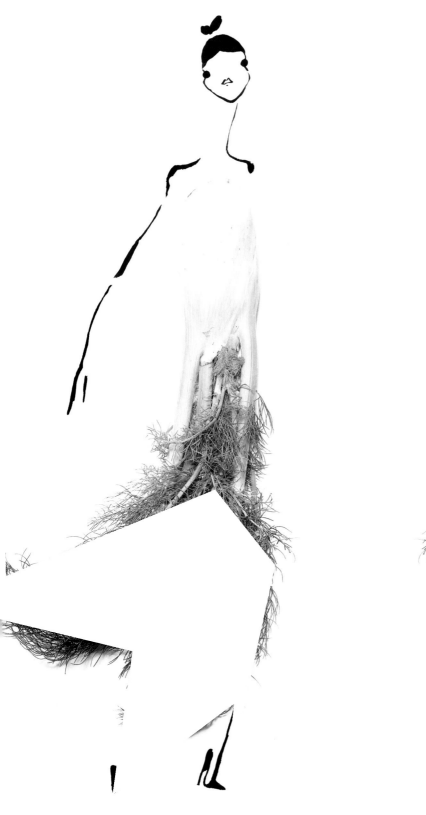

friends in fennel

i get by with a little

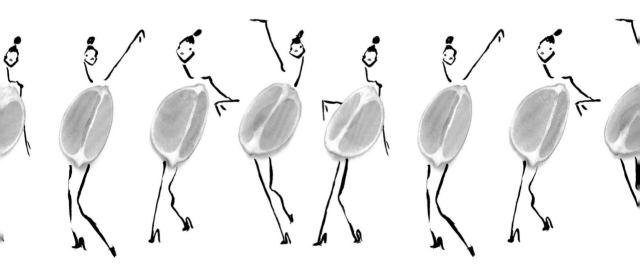

help from my friends

Romanesque, oh!

always pack a party 'choke

blue

BLUEBERRIES. BLACKBERRIES. MUSSELS.

dressed to impress

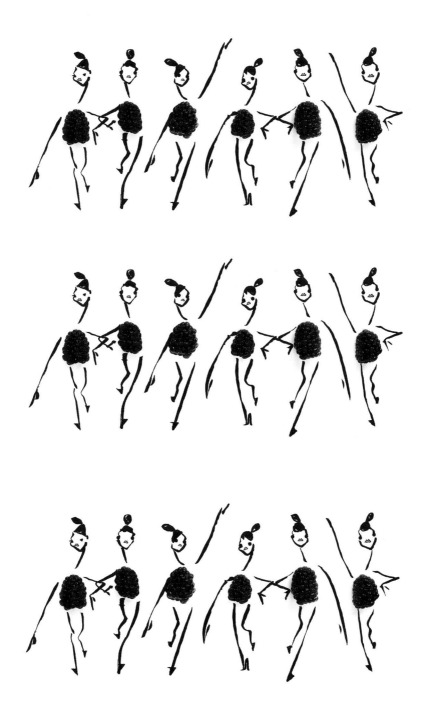

pink

CRANBERRY. DRAGON FRUIT. FIG. EGGPLANT.
WATERMELON RADISH. LYCHEE. POMEGRANATE.
PURPLE CAULIFLOWER. PASSION FRUIT. GRAPE-
FRUIT. RED ONION.

getting figgy

with it

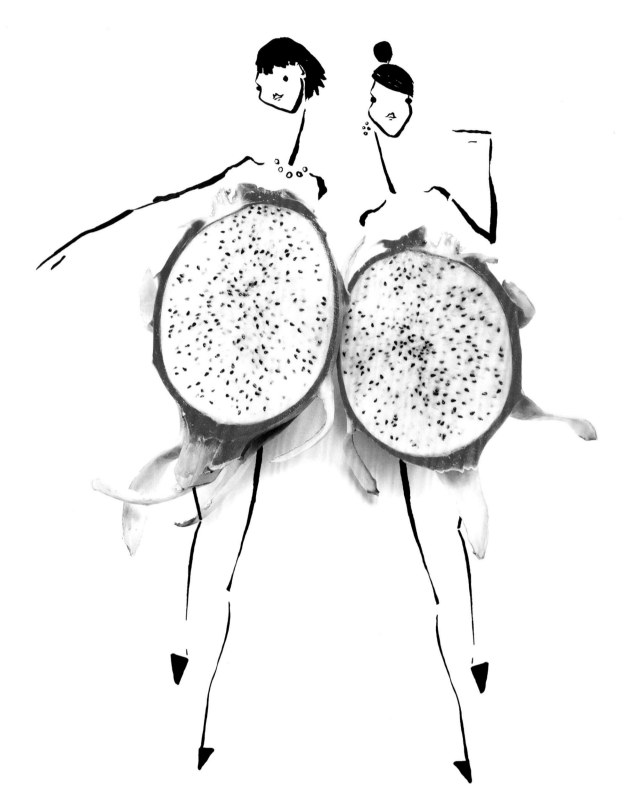

think pink

nude

OYSTERS. MAITAKE MUSHROOM. PASTA. UNI.

TRUMPET MUSHROOM. CROISSANT. CAULIFLOWER.

PEAR. OLIVES. GARLIC. COFFEE. CHOCOLATE.

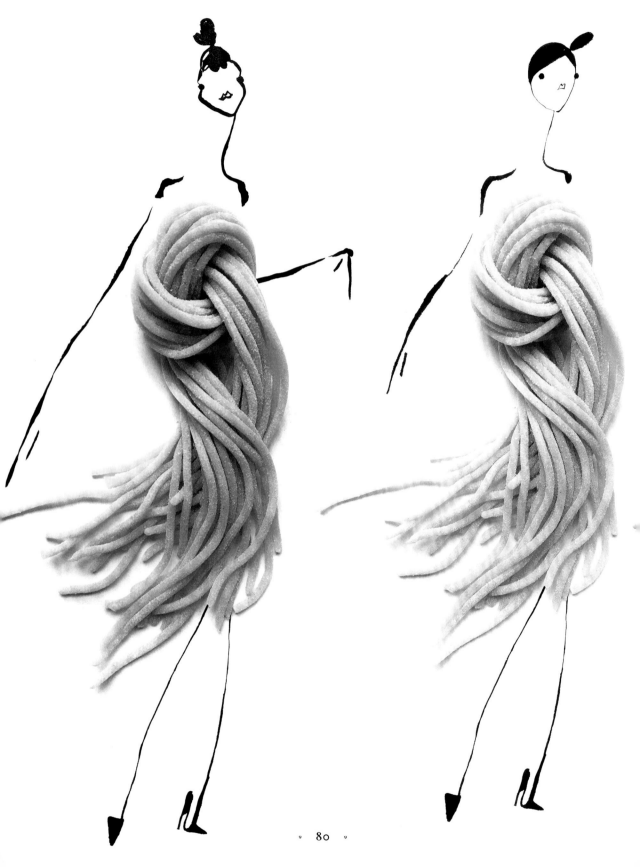

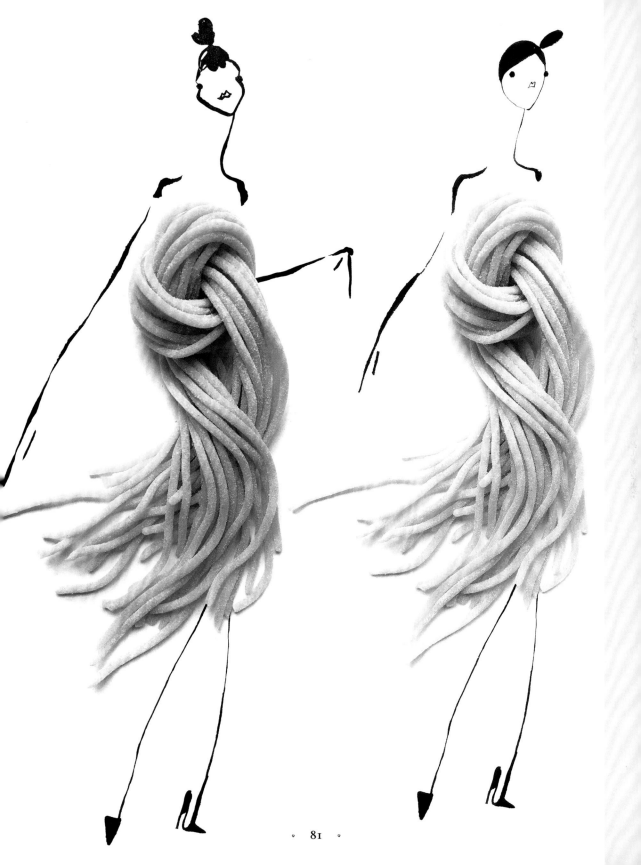

work the shroom

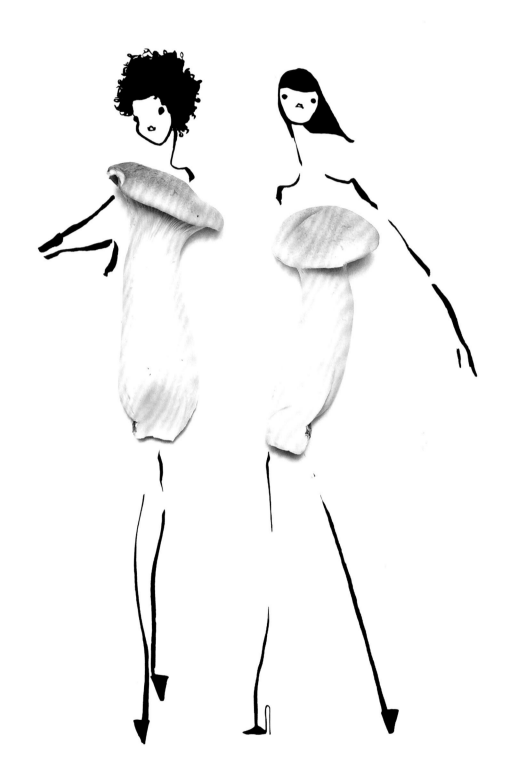

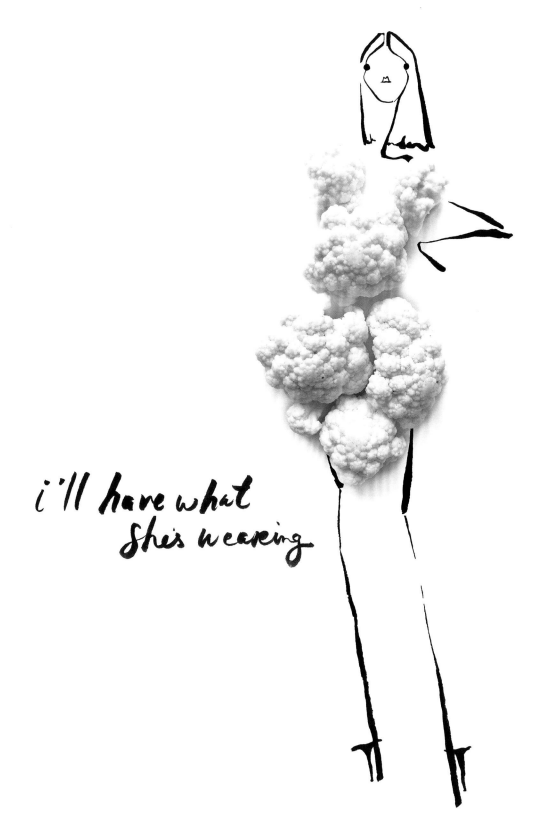

i'll have what
she's wearing

liberté, egalité, pâtisserie!

des urchins

First published in the United States of America in 2018 by
Rizzoli International Publications, Inc.
300 Park Avenue South, New York, NY 10010
www.rizzoliusa.com

Editor: Ellen Nidy
Design by Sarah Chiarot

2018 2019 2020 2021 2022 / 10 9 8 7 6 5 4 3 2 1

ISBN-13: 978-0-8478-6231-3

Library of Congress Control Number: 2017956507

Printed and bound in China

Distributed to the U.S. trade by Random House

to eat is human, to dress, divine